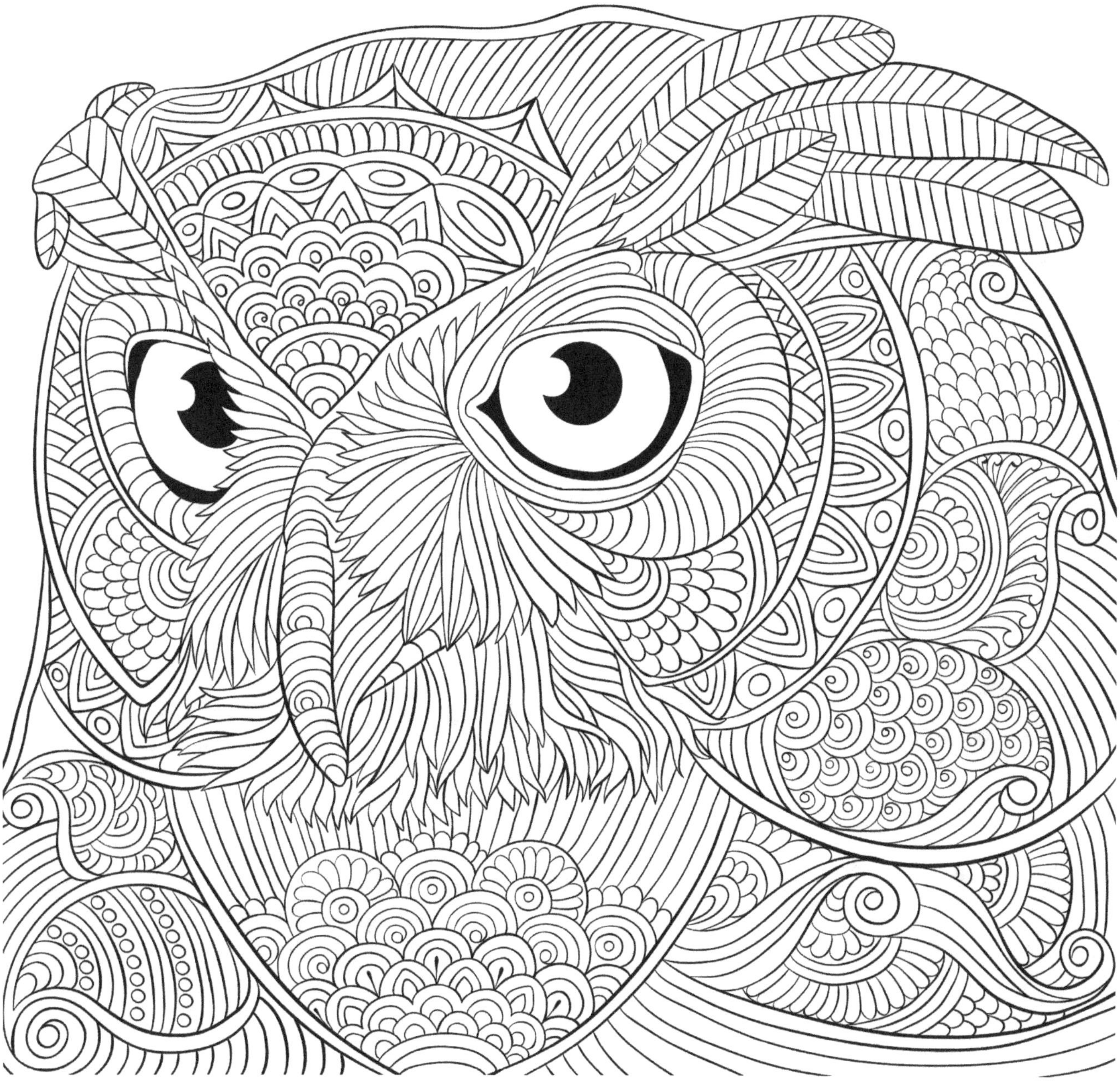

ISBN: 978-1523394036

Illustrated by:
   Mandala & Caricature Illustration
   Joshua Lazana Lagman and Jade Villaremo

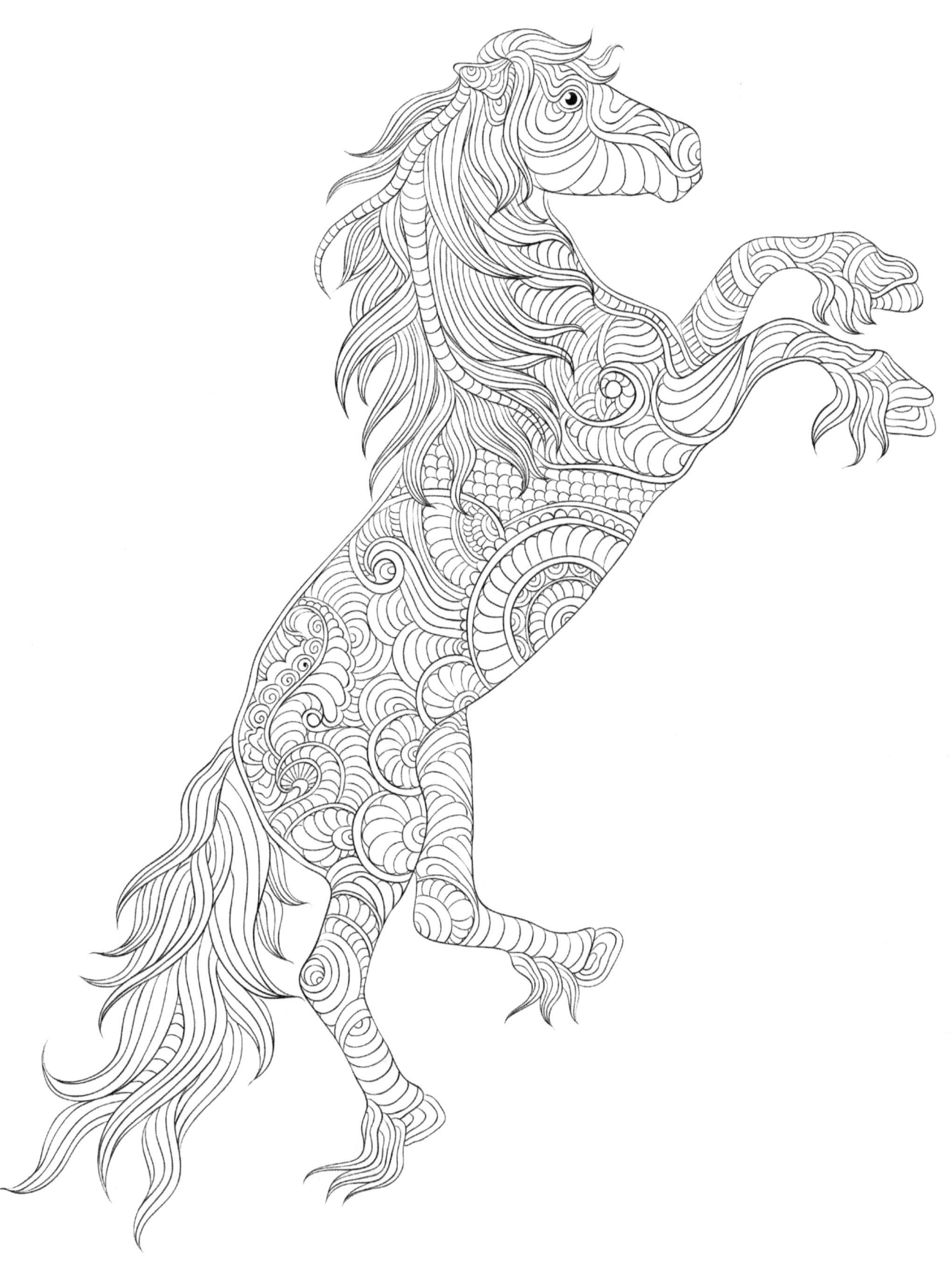

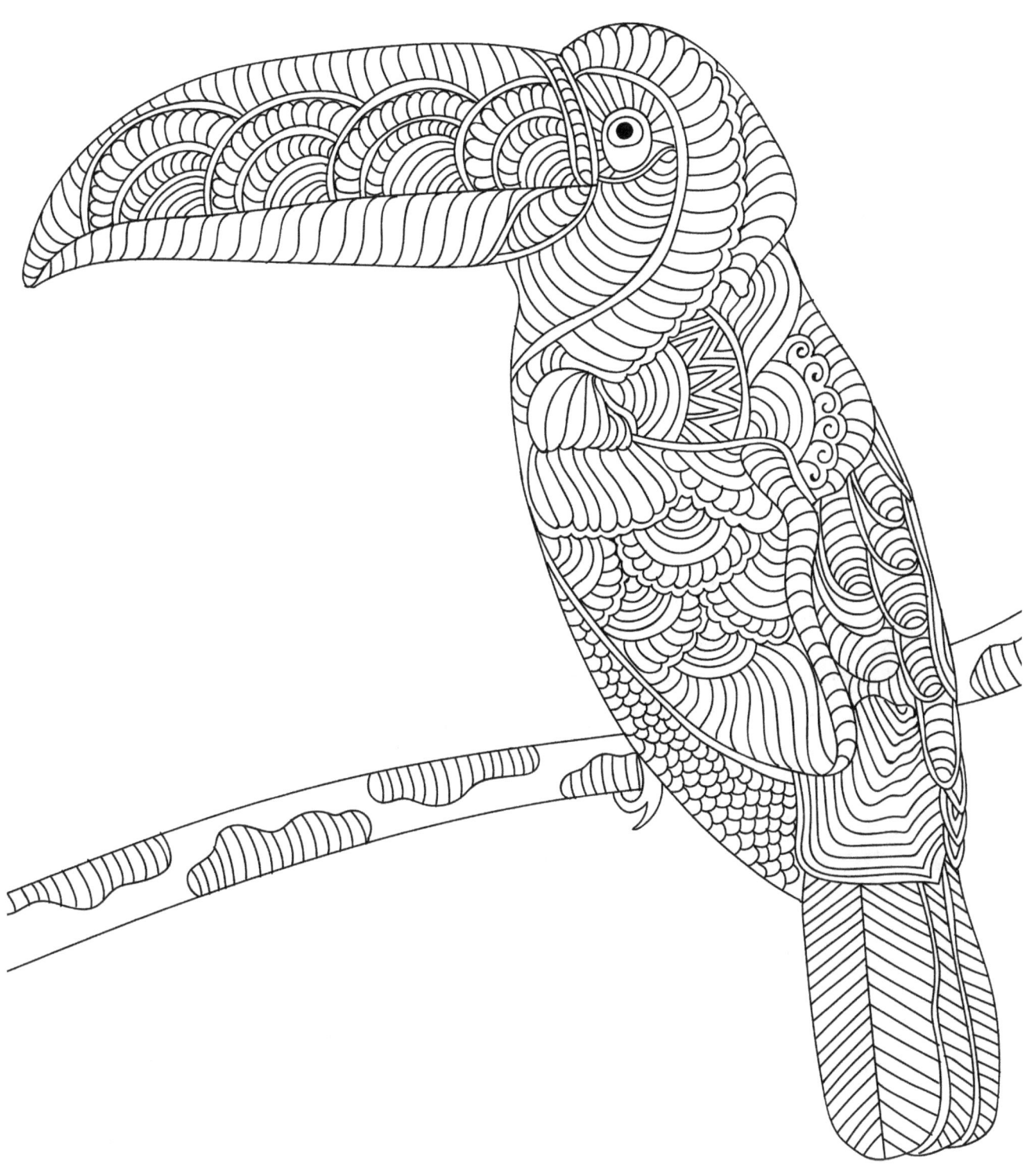

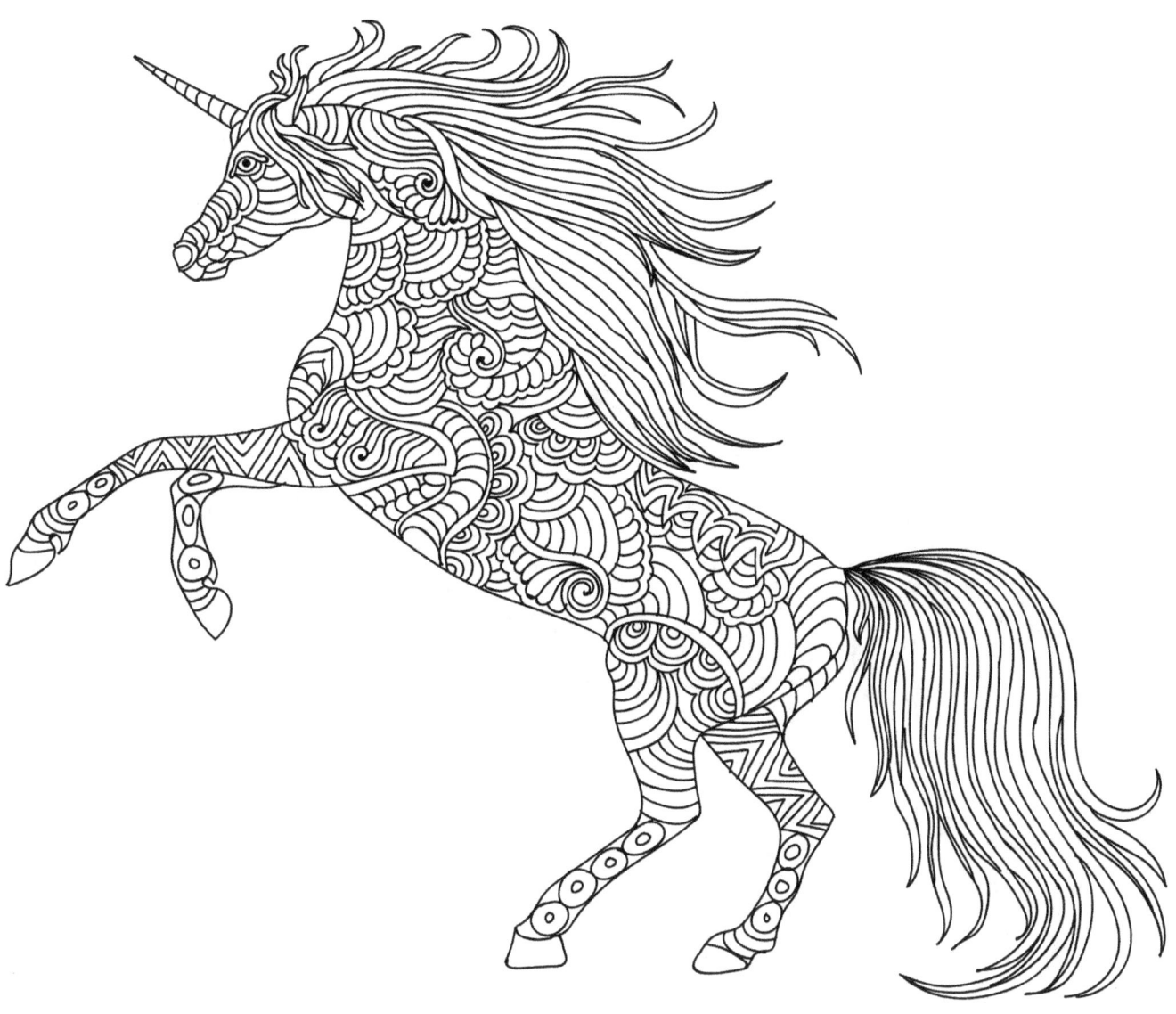

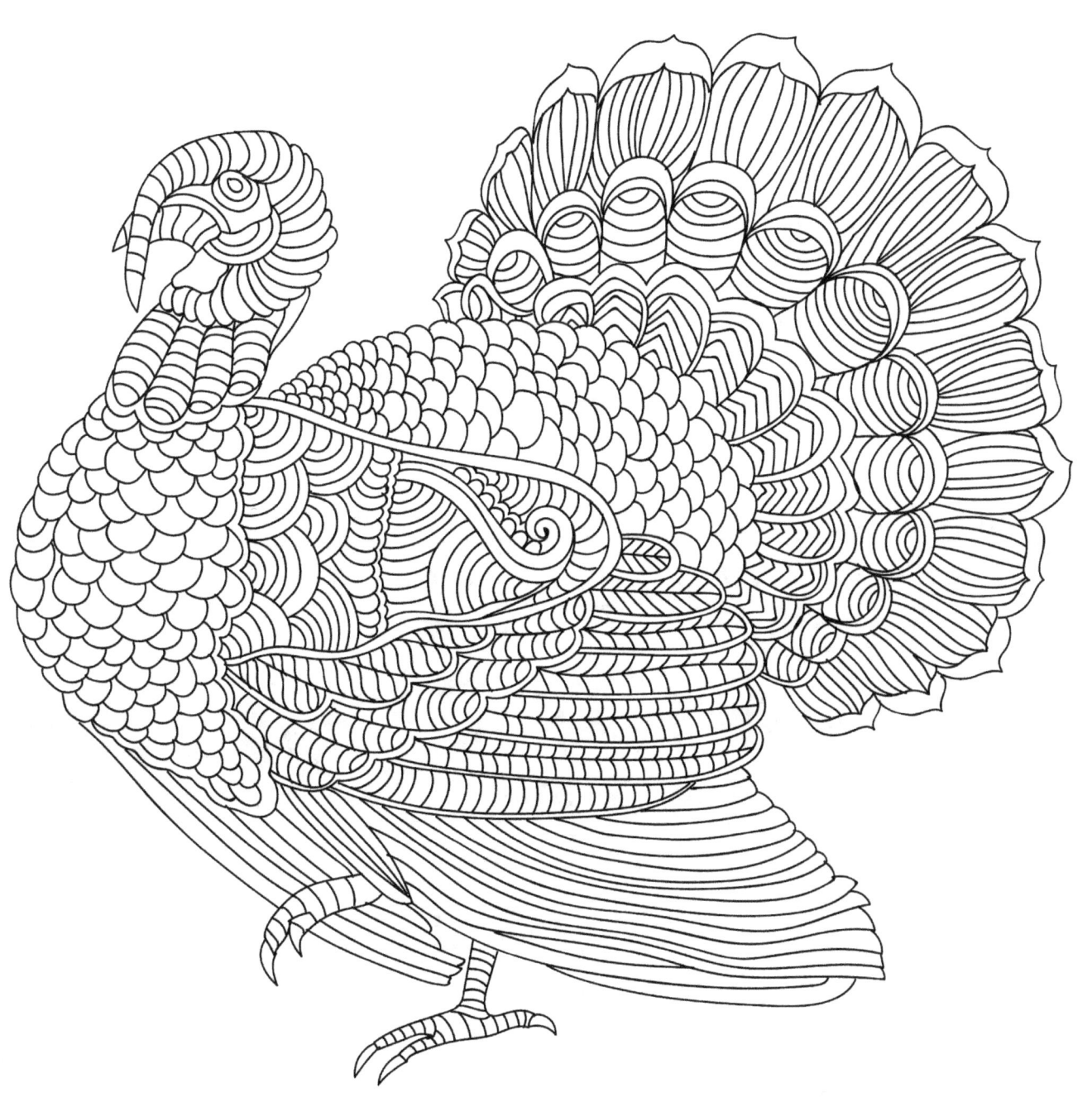

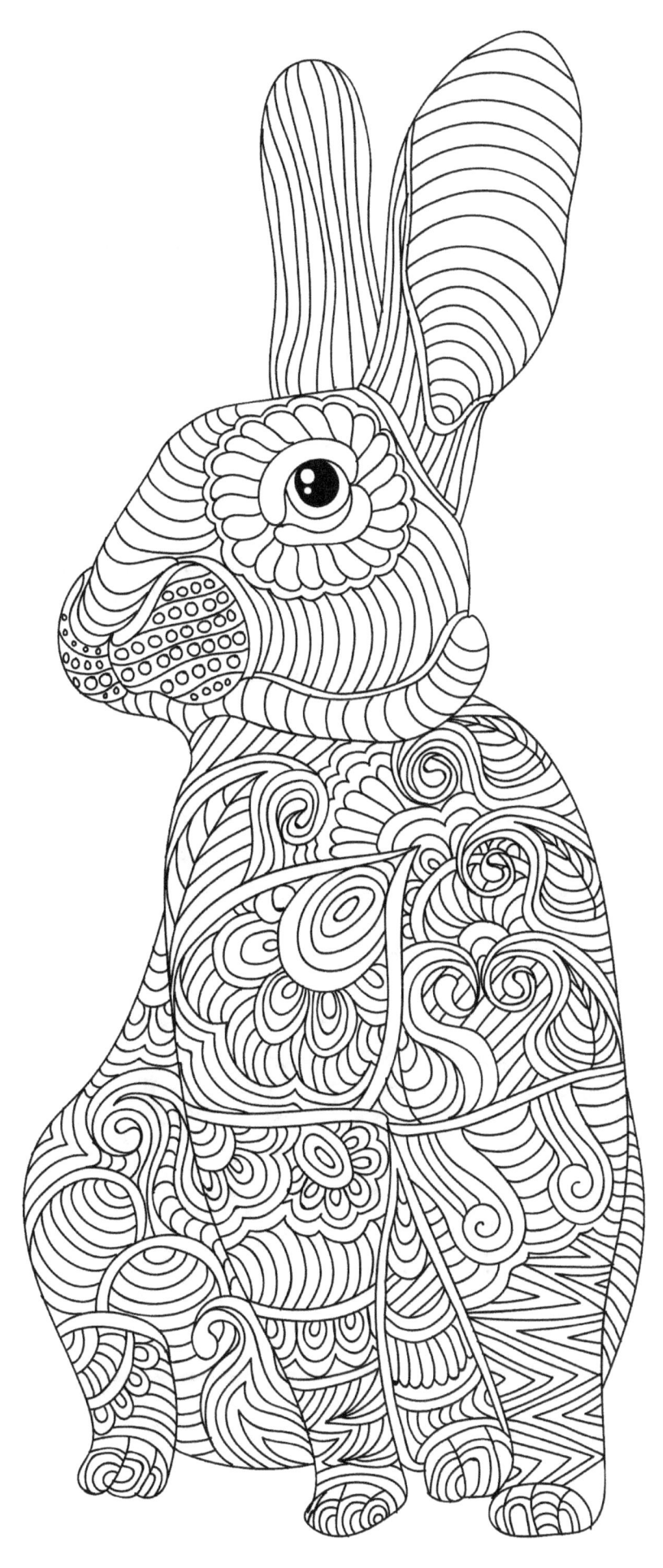

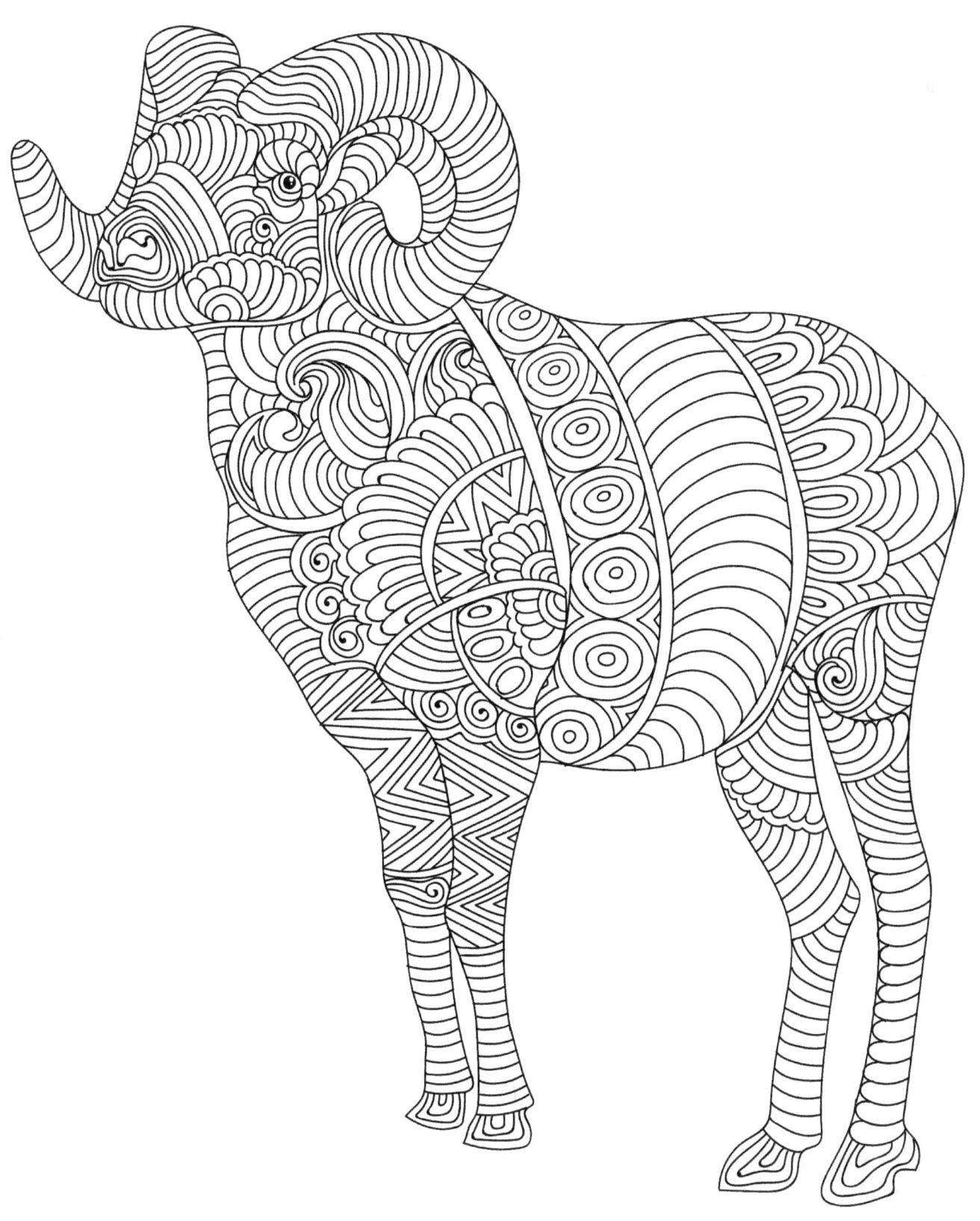

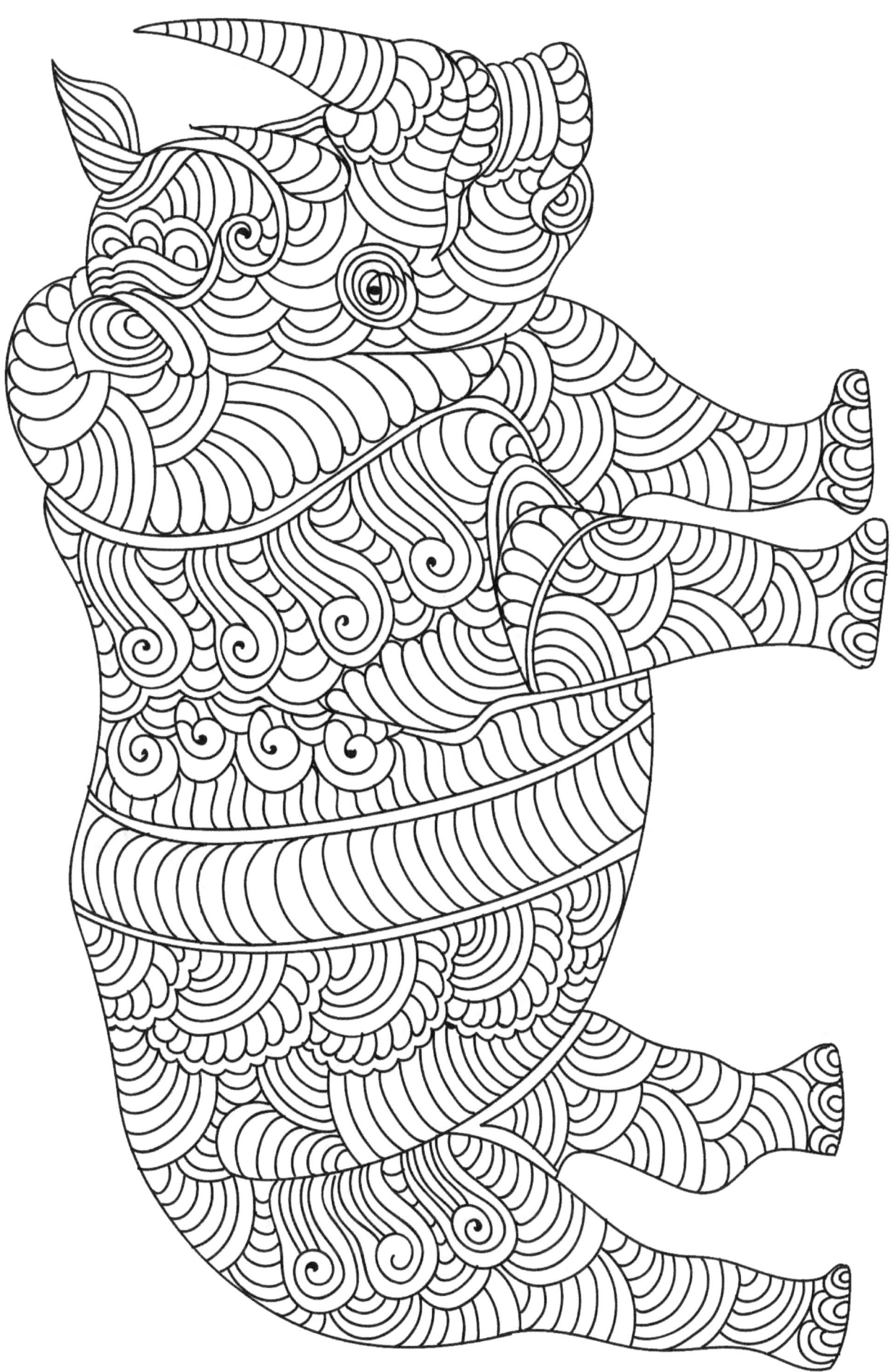

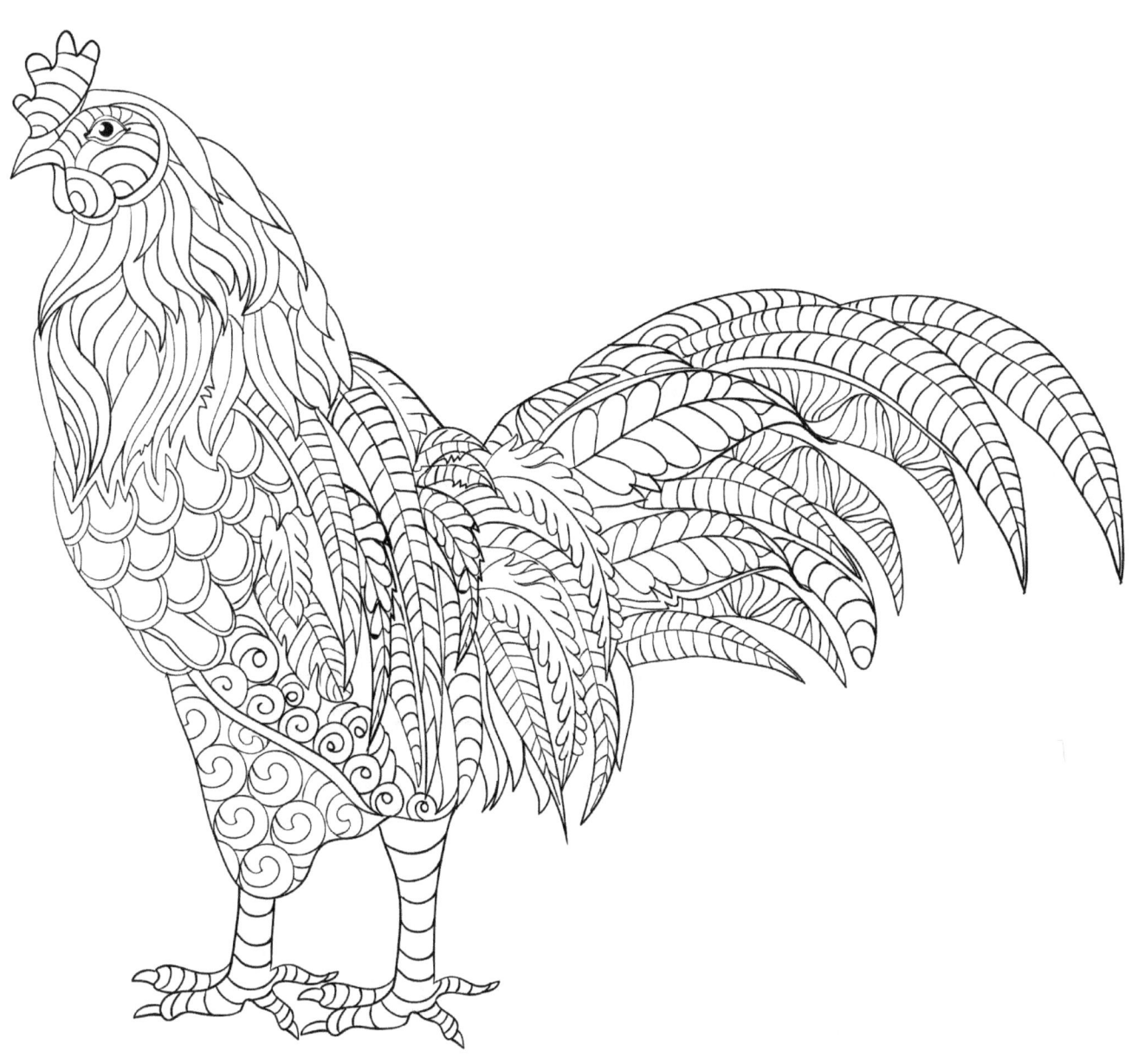

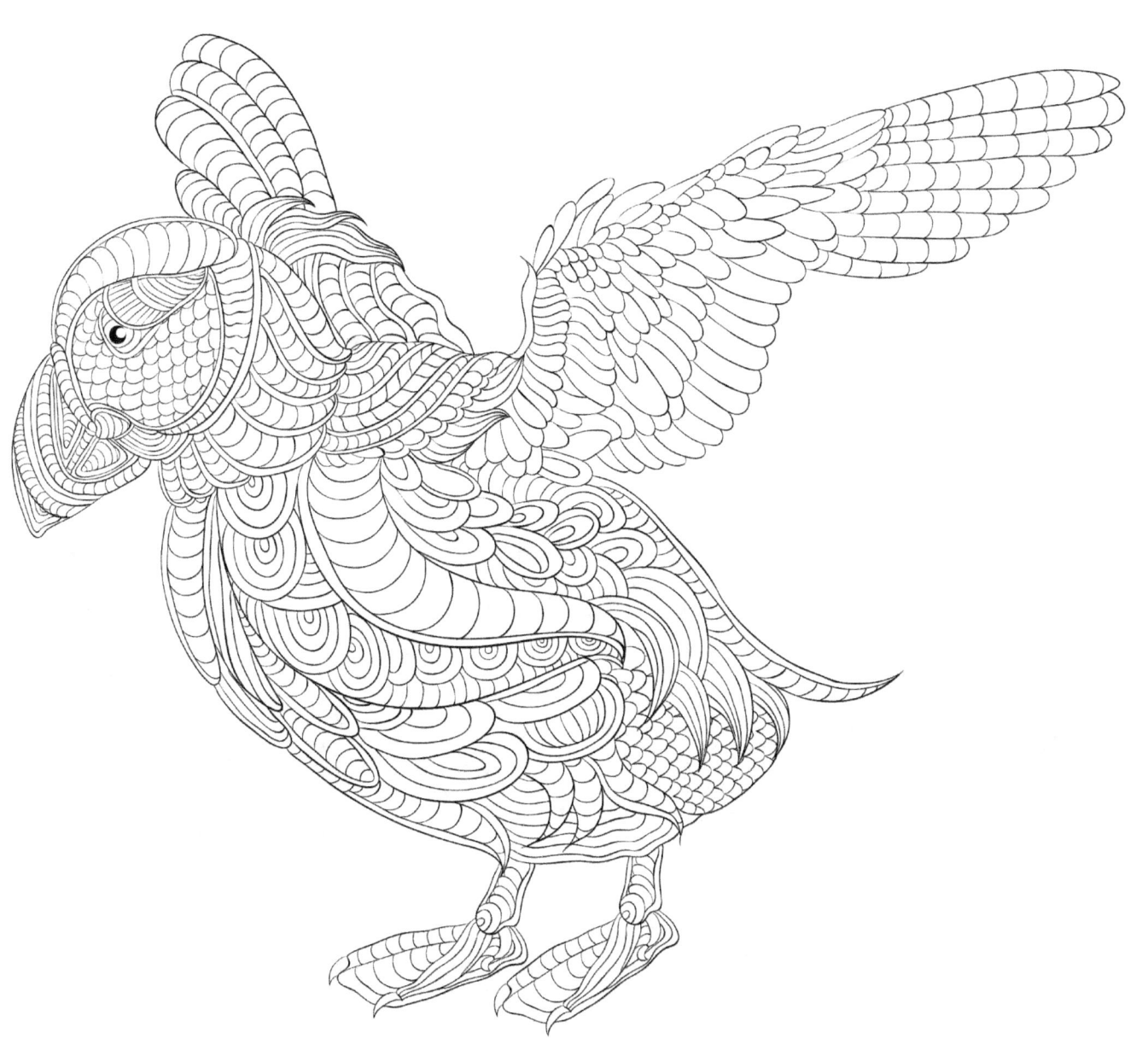

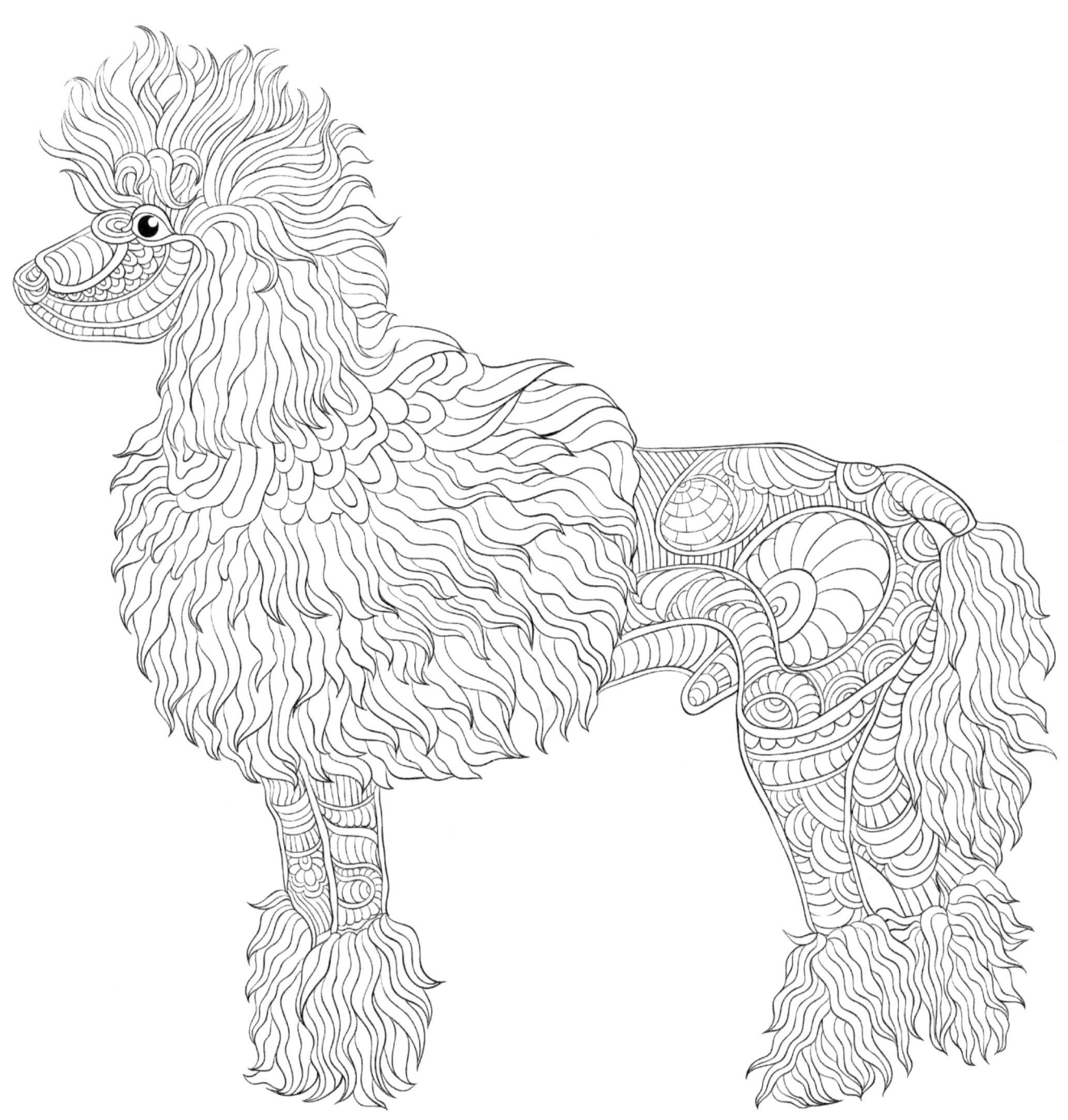

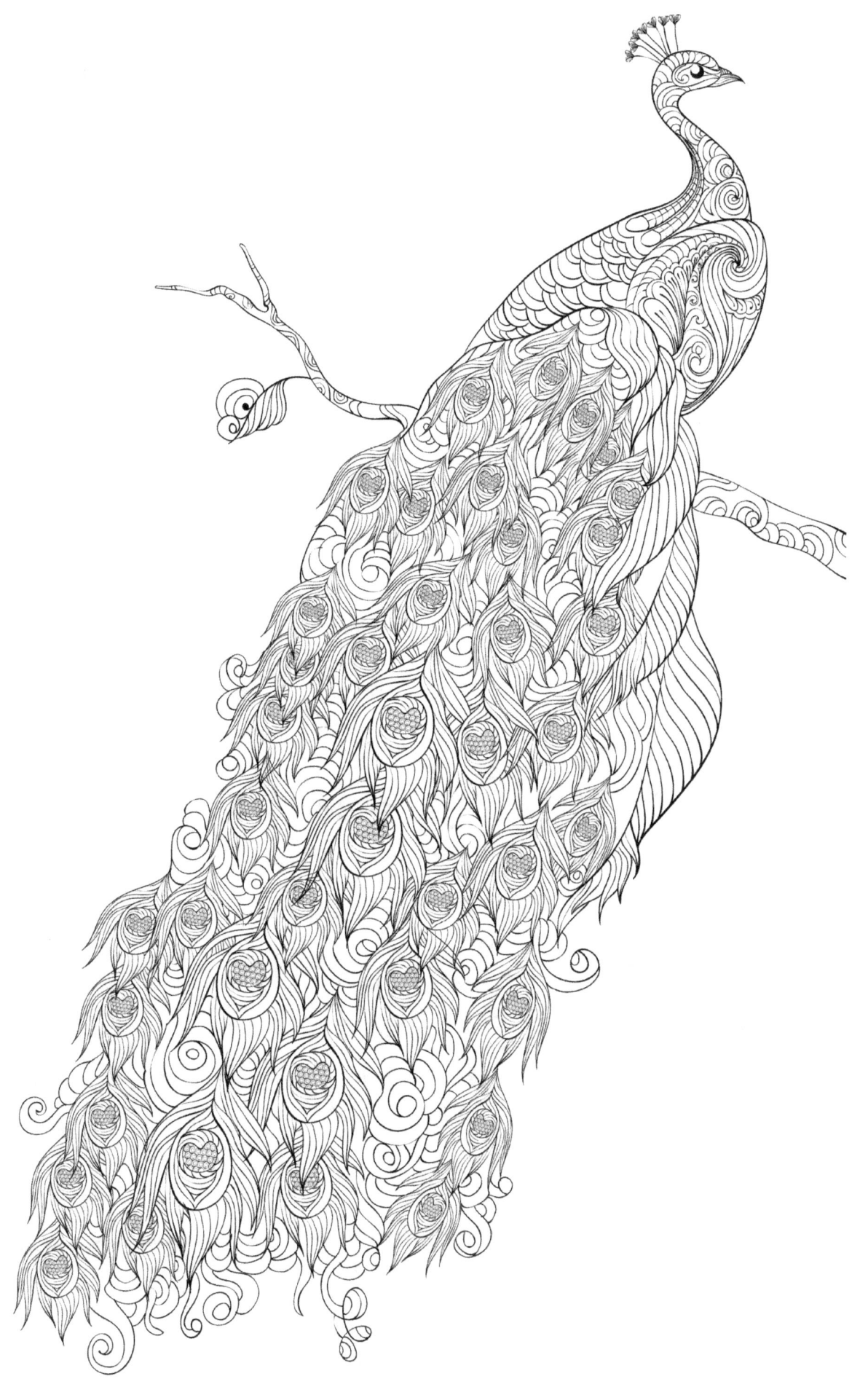

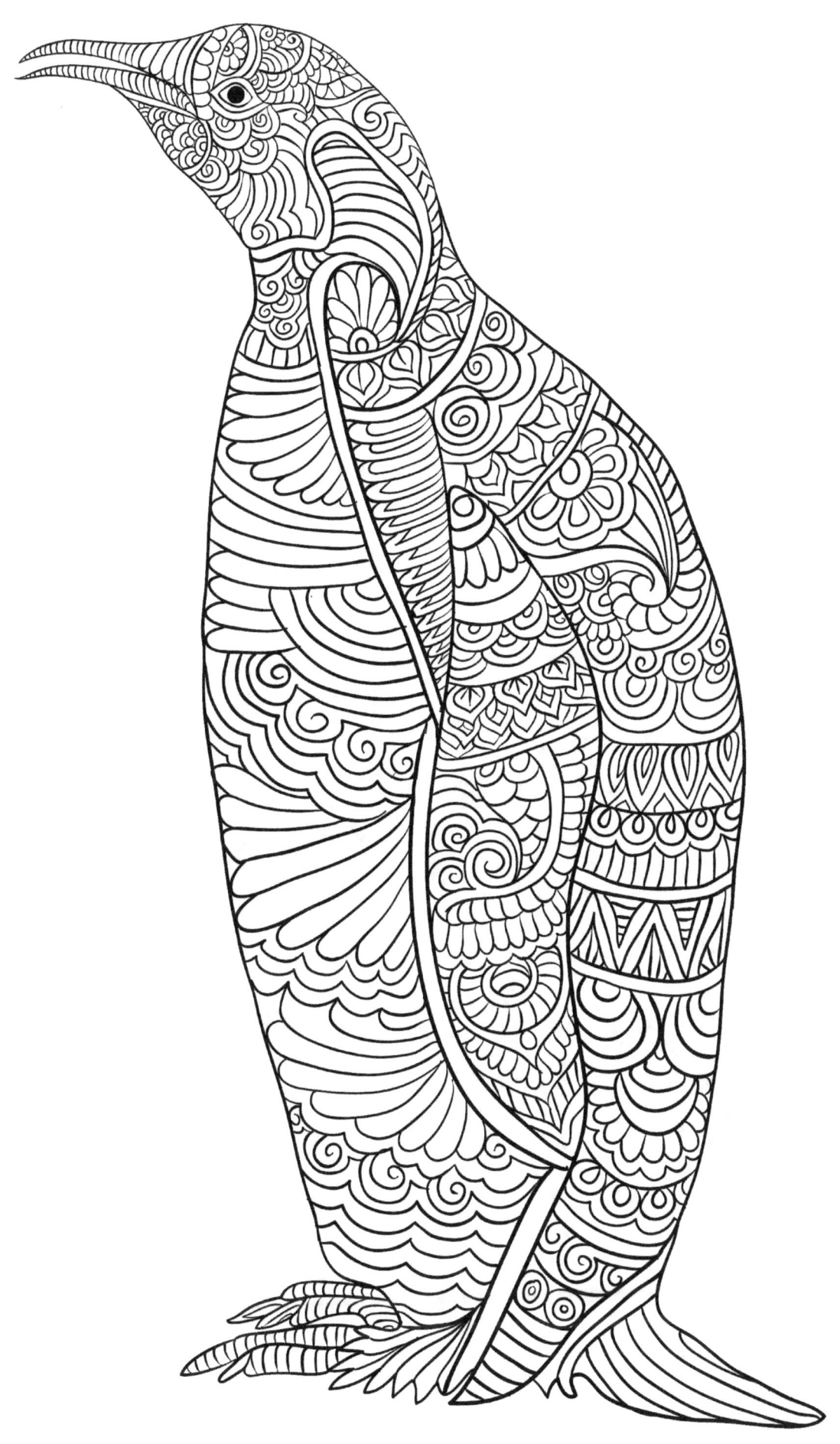

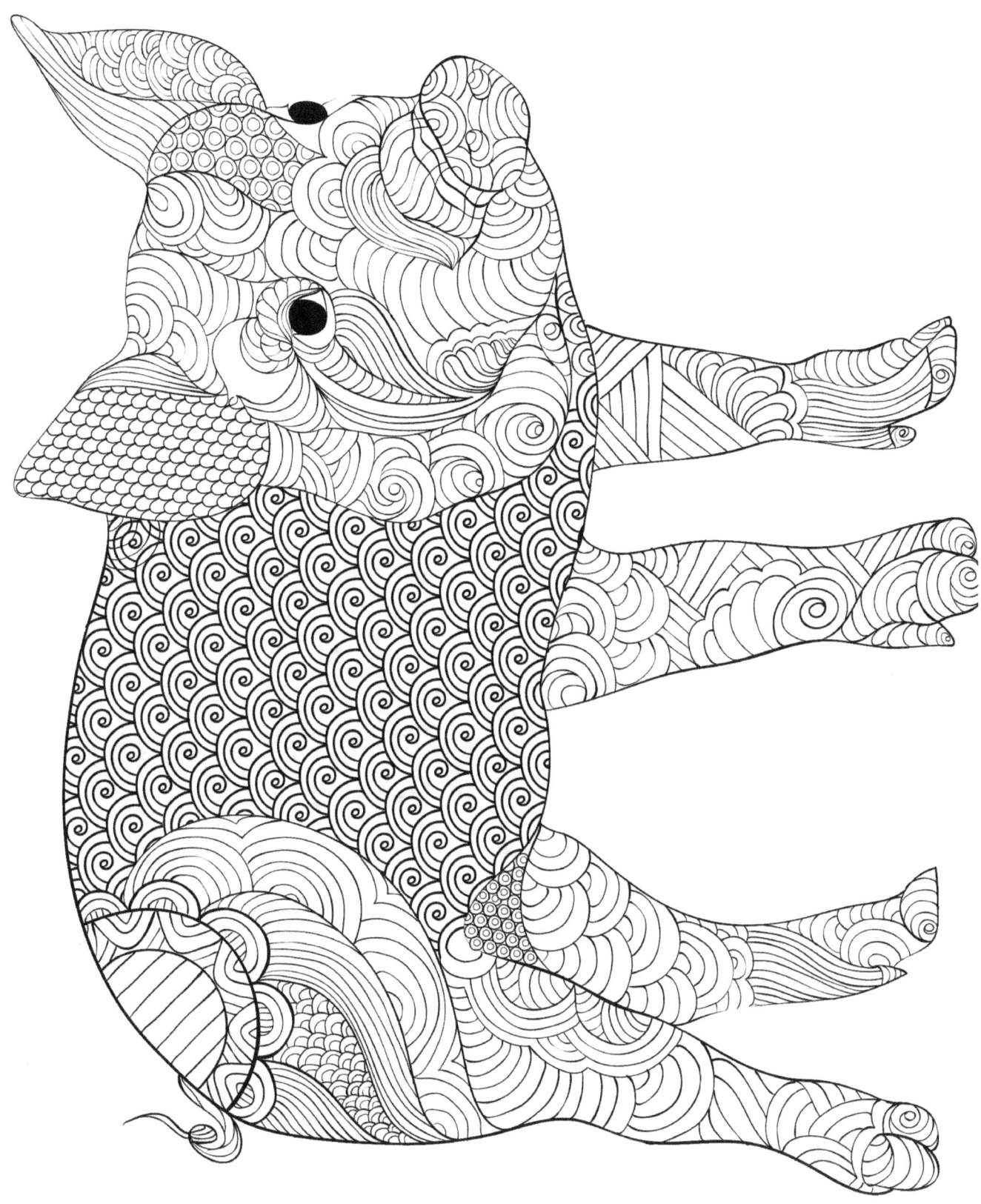

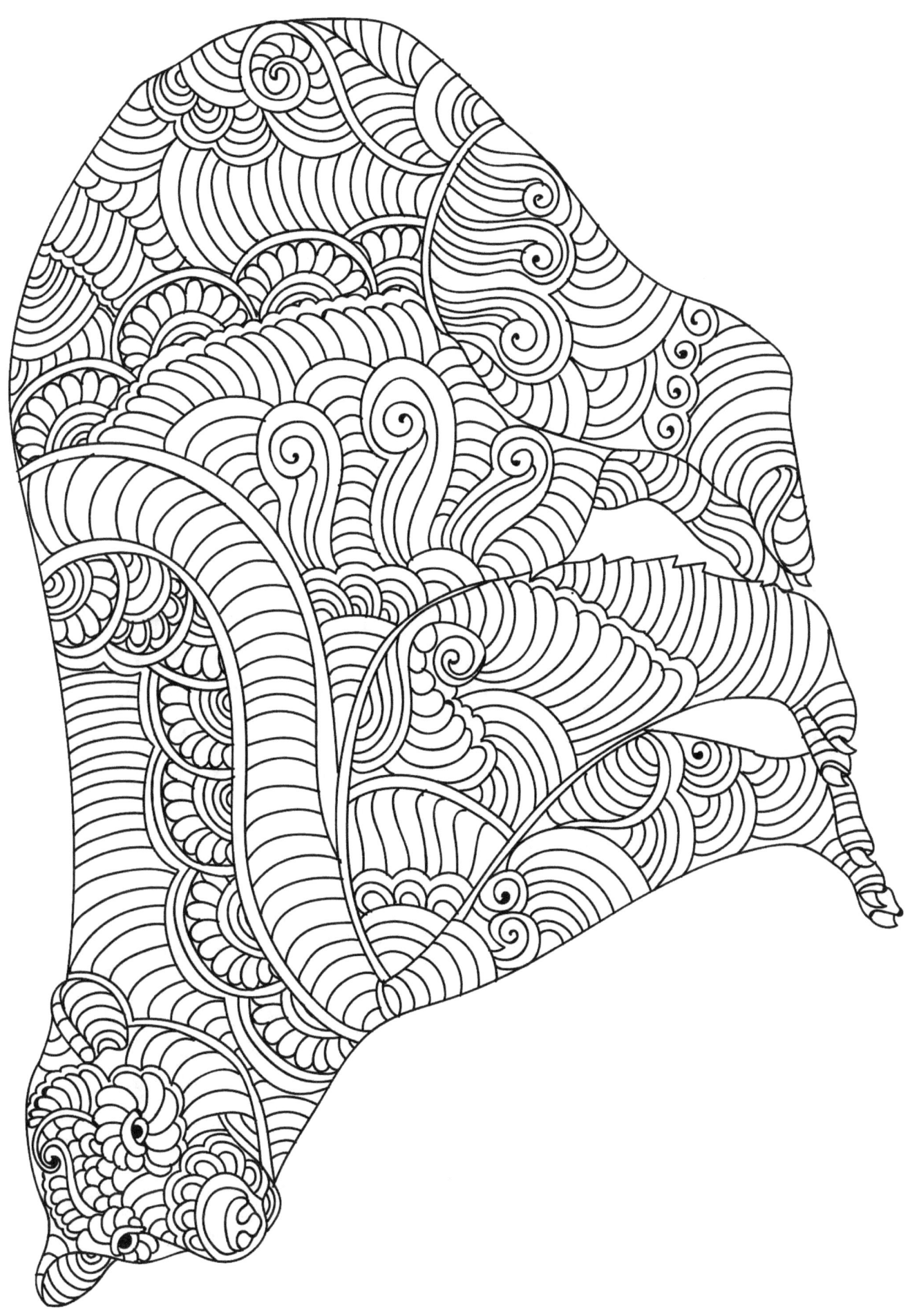

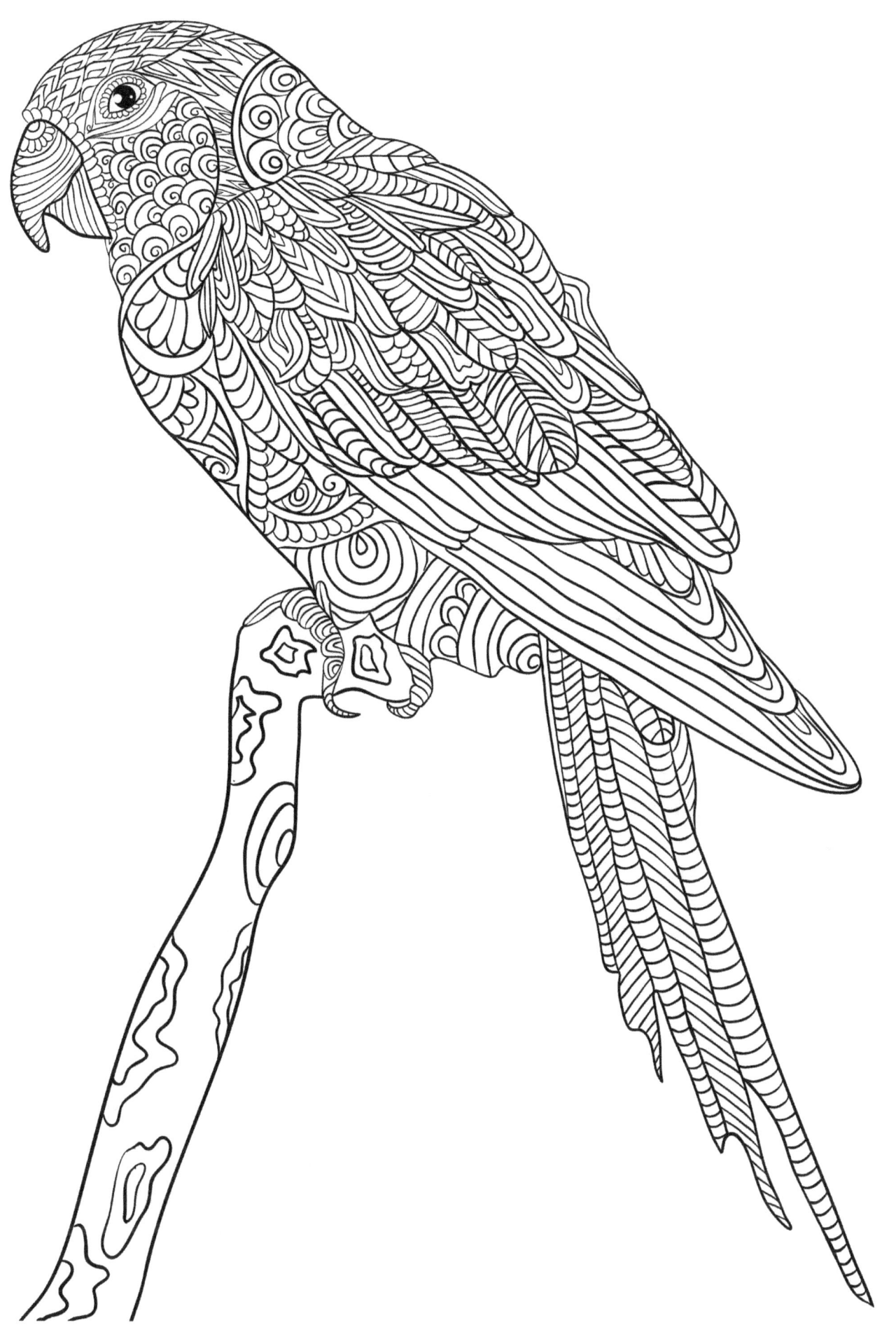

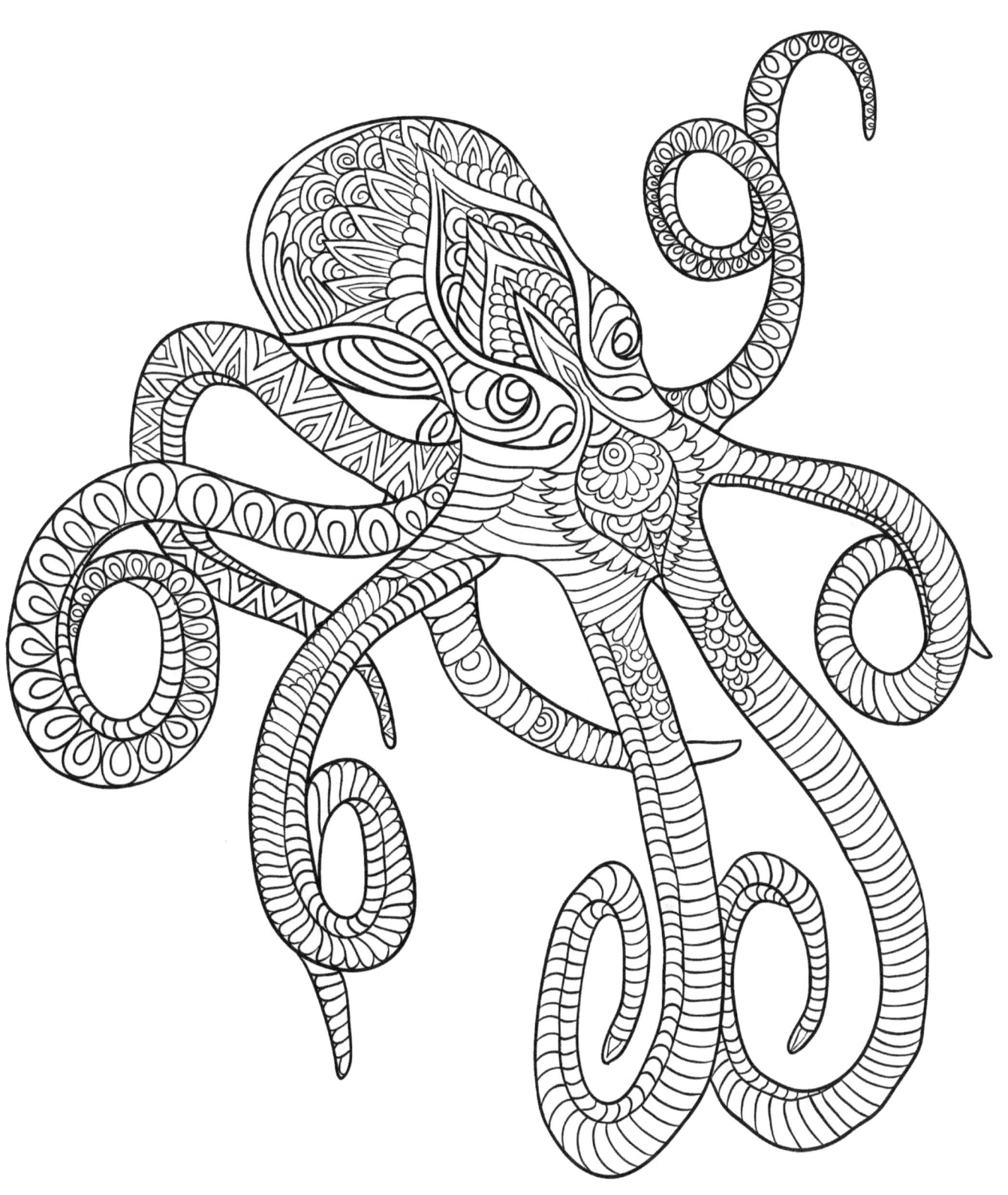

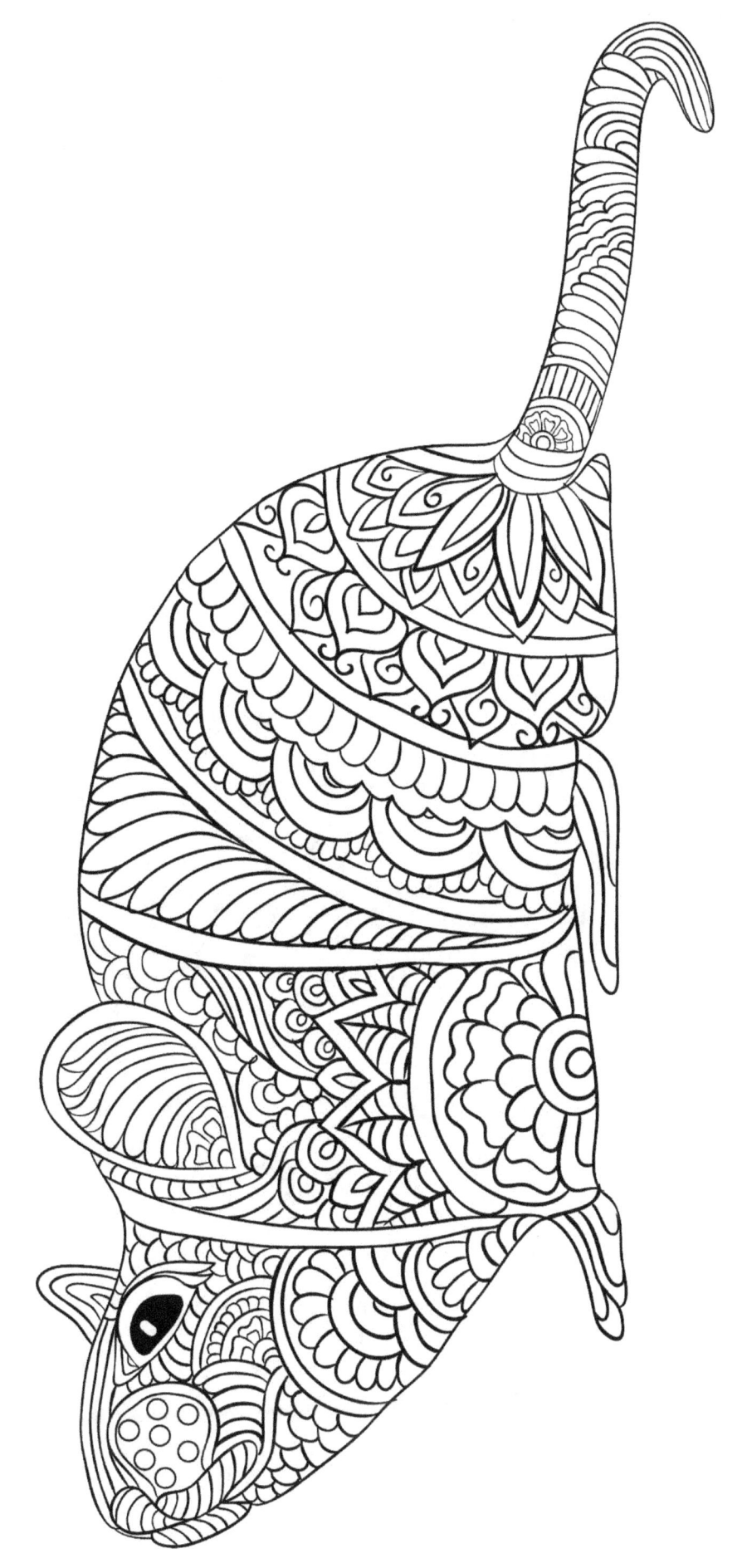

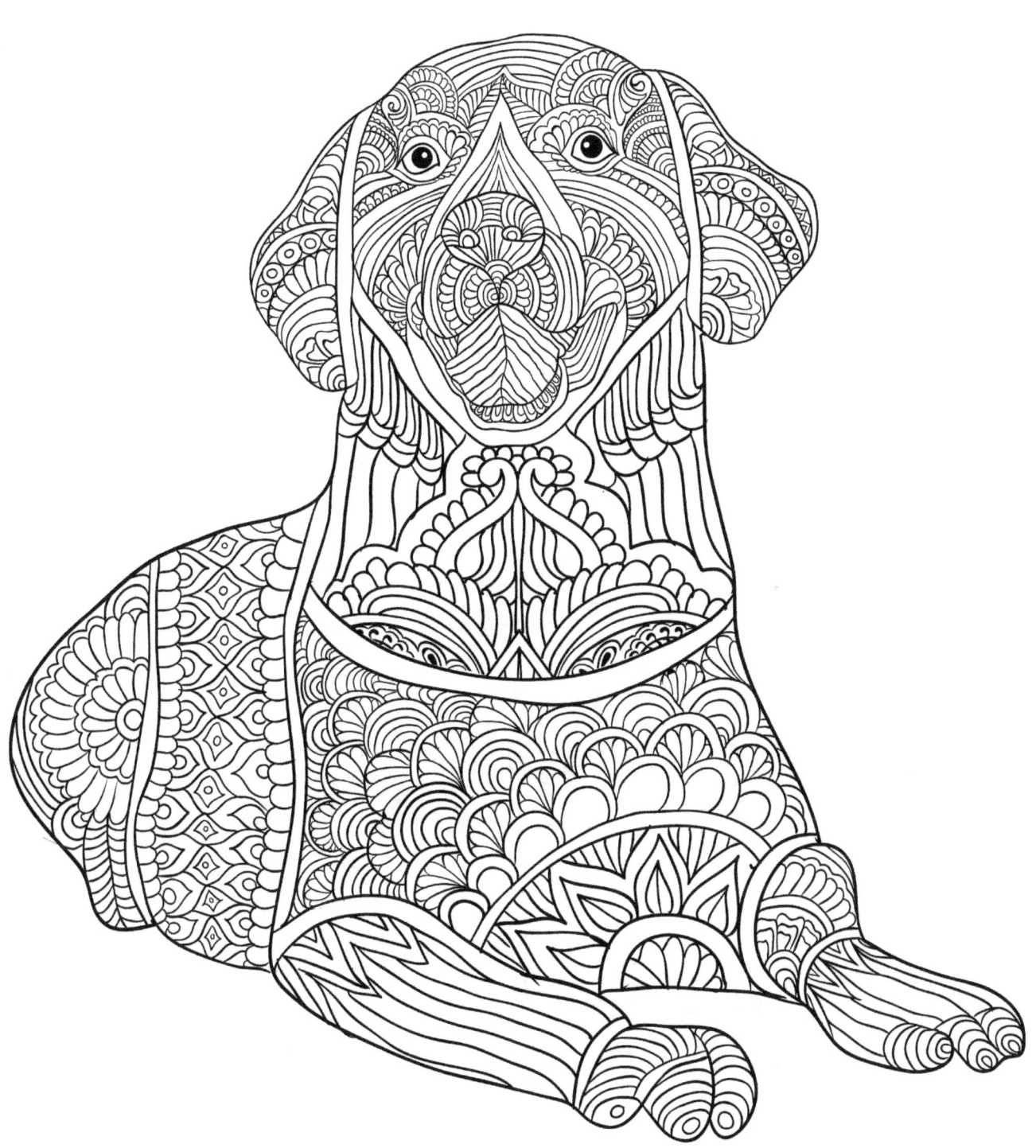

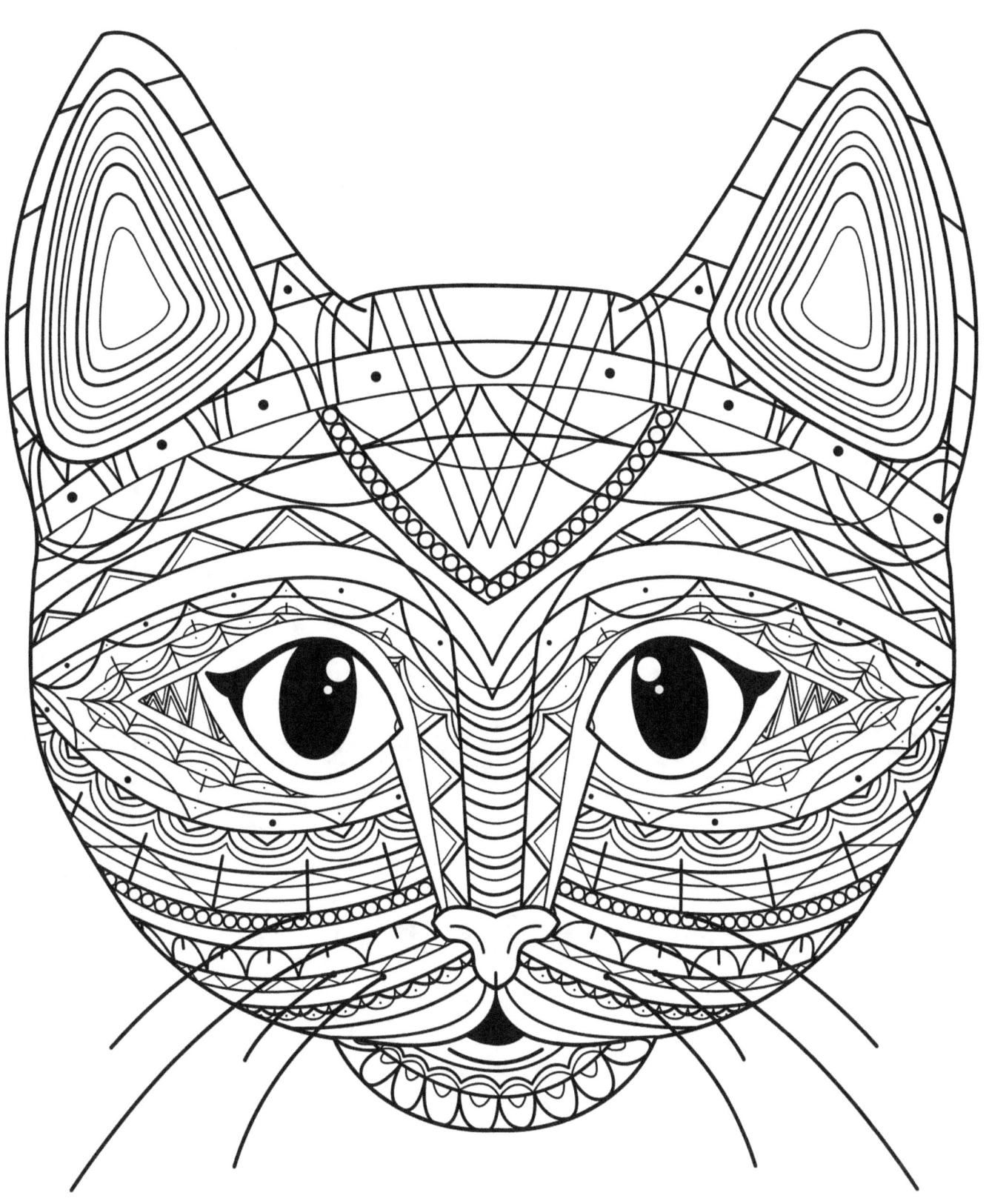

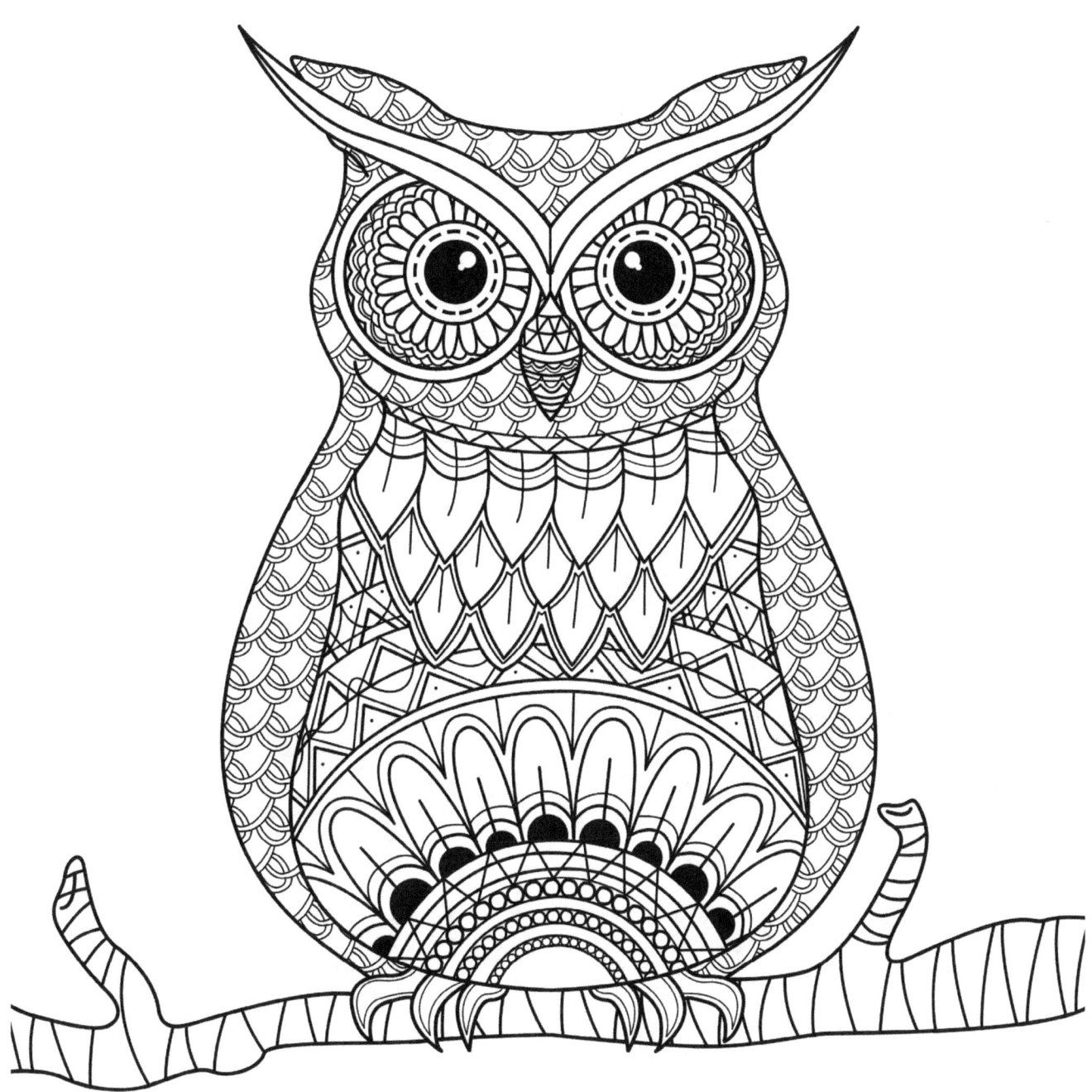

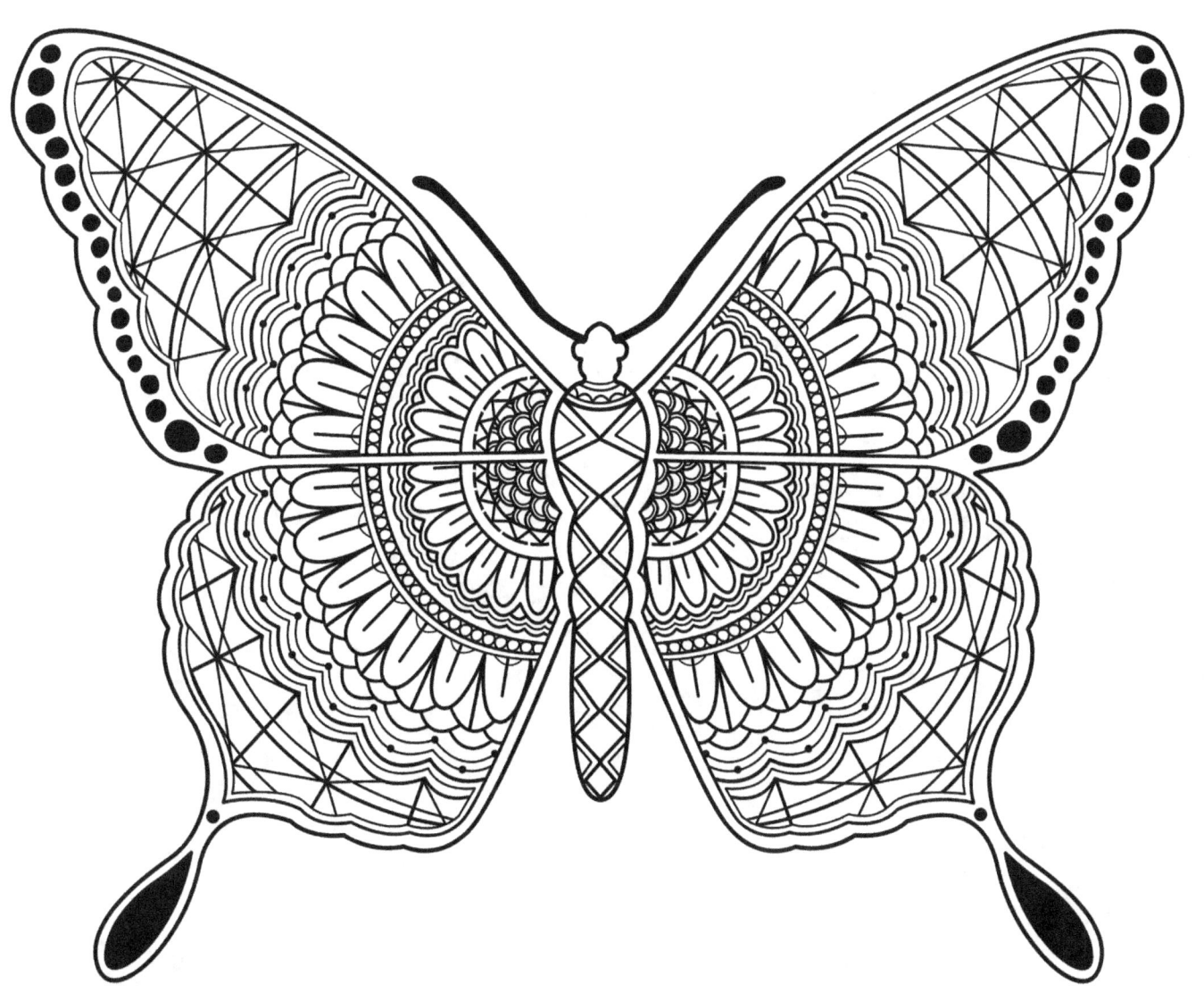

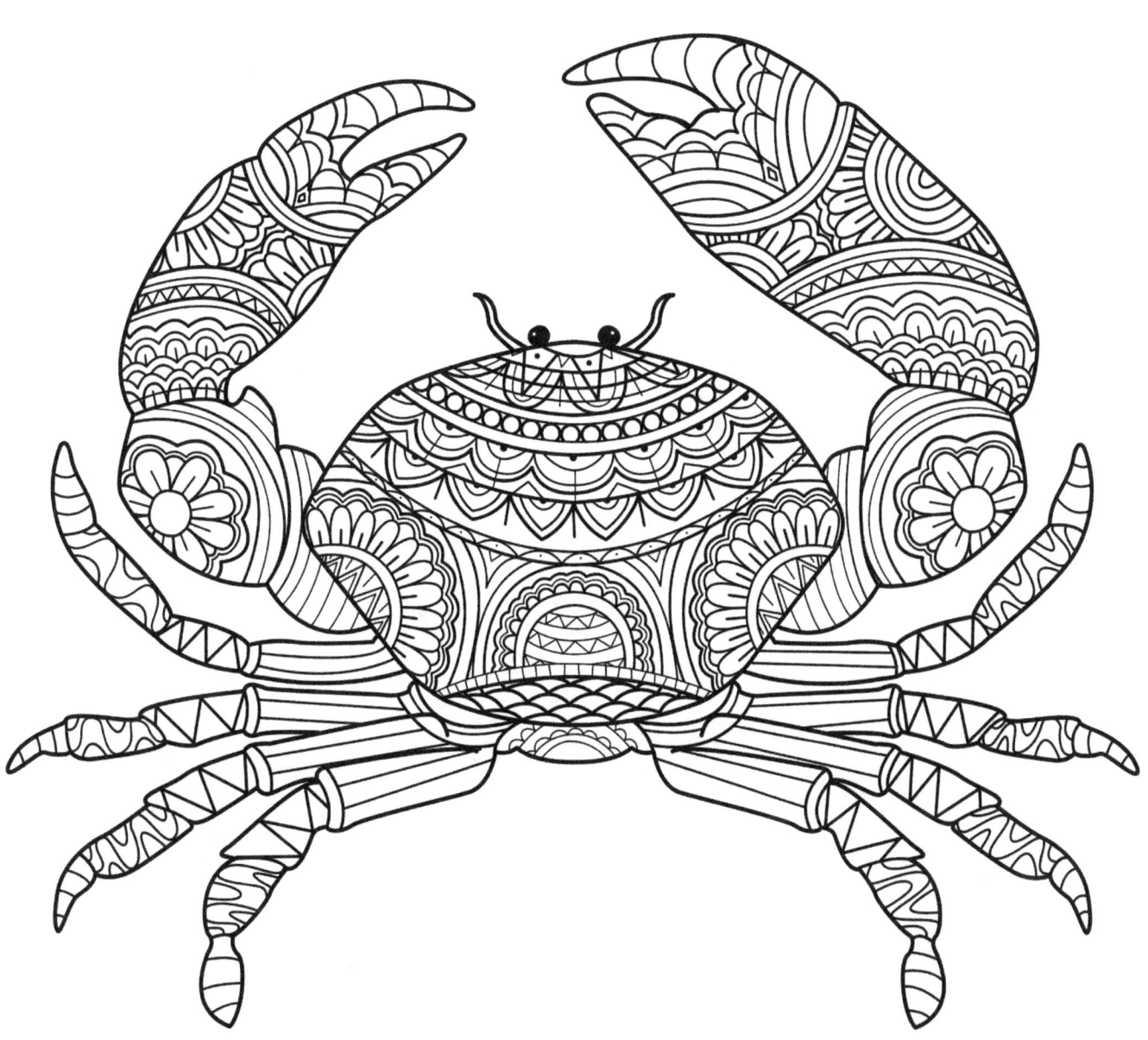

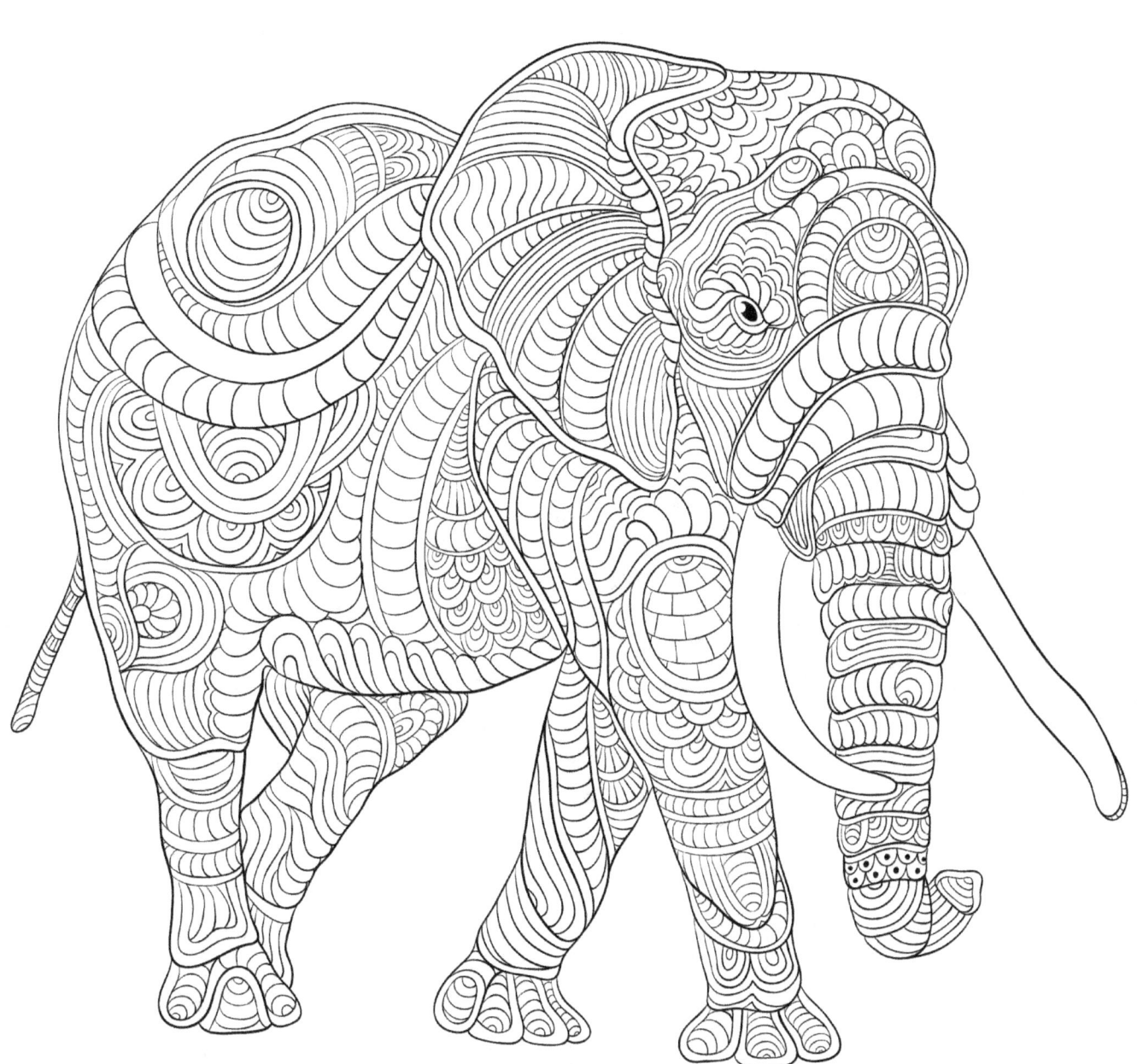

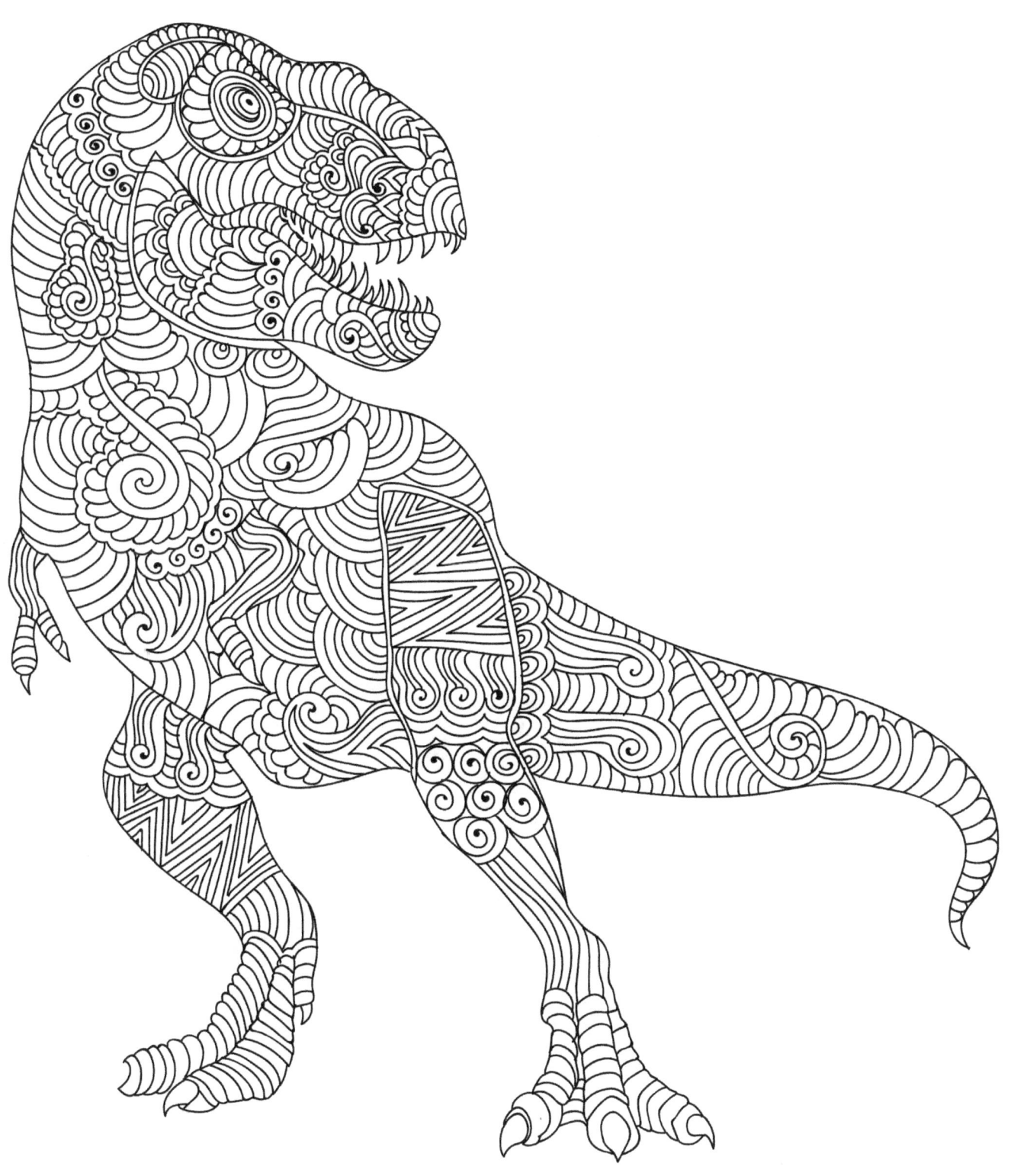

Free Bonus Book

$3.99 value electronic coloring book, easy to print out. Download your FREE book now:

http://CoolAdultColoringBooks.com

More: Check our website above for new books and special promotion deals...

www.ingramcontent.com/pod-product-compliance
Lightning Source LLC
Chambersburg PA
CBHW081132180526
45170CB00008B/3075